HOW TO HELP STUDENTS REMAIN SEATED

Saul Axelrod

HOW TO IMPROVE CLASSROOM BEHAVIOR SERIES

SERIES EDITORS

Saul Axelrod
Steven C. Mathews

8700 Shoal Creek Boulevard
Austin, Texas 78757-6897
800/897-3202 Fax 800/397-7633
www.proedinc.com

© 2003 by PRO-ED, Inc.
8700 Shoal Creek Boulevard
Austin, Texas 78757-6897
800/897-3202 Fax 800/397-7633
www.proedinc.com

All rights reserved. No part of the material protected by this copyright notice may be reproduced or used in any form or by any means, electronic or mechanical, including photocopying, recording, or by any information storage and retrieval system, without prior written permission of the copyright owner.

Library of Congress Cataloging-in-Publication Data

Axelrod, Saul.
    How to help students remain seated / Saul Axelrod.
      p. cm. — (How to improve classroom behavior series)
    Includes bibliographical references.
    ISBN 0-89079-912-1
    1. Classroom management. 2. Behavior modification. I. Title. II. Series.

LB3013.A94 2003
371.102'4—dc21

                                        2002035795

This book is designed in Minion and Gill Sans.

Printed in the United States of America

1 2 3 4 5 6 7 8 9 10   06 05 04 03 02

CONTENTS

Foreword • v

Preface to Series • vii

Introduction 1

Steps for Modifying Behavior 1

Importance of Being Positive 8

Procedures To Help Students Remain Seated 15

Pointers for Successfully Modifying Behavior 24

Final Examination • 35

Answer Key • 43

Further Readings • 45

About the Author • 47

FOREWORD

Having spent several years as a classroom teacher, as a principal of both regular and special education students, and as an educational researcher, it has long been apparent to me that there is a need for materials that provide quick solutions to specific classroom problems. The *How To Improve Classroom Behavior Series* edited by Saul Axelrod and Steven C. Mathews fills that need. Although there have been a number of excellent research studies and texts that present effective classroom management techniques, the beauty of this series is that the authors have used their own experiences and surveyed the literature to present effective procedures that efficiently guide teachers toward solutions of common classroom management problems.

The value of such a series should be apparent. Teachers faced with particular problems, such as students who are disruptive or who bully or tease, can consult the series for solutions. Ideally these books will be found on a bookshelf in the teachers' lounge. Without having to search through professional journals or cumbersome texts, teachers will easily be able to focus on the particular behavior that is a topic of concern. Principals, school psychologists, counselors, and other professionals to whom teachers sometimes refer students with problem behaviors, will also find these texts useful in providing solutions for teachers. It also should prove extremely helpful, especially to beginning teachers, when a principal or psychologist can provide a simple, uncluttered text that tells the teacher exactly what to do in certain problem situations.

The booklets in the series are presented in such a way that they help the user to clearly define the behavior of concern and then to implement step-by-step programs that deal effectively with that behavior. Because the booklets are written in straightforward, nontechnical language, teachers will not become bogged down in trying to understand psychological jargon or complex procedures.

Saul Axelrod is a respected researcher and author. He has published more than 60 research articles and book chapters on behavior and eight books that deal with classroom problems. An excellent writer, he has served on the editorial boards of ten prominent psychological and educational journals. As a licensed psychologist and professor of special education, he has wide experience in instructing teachers in the use of classroom management techniques. Due to his extensive experience and many professional contacts, he and his coeditor were able to select authors well qualified to write each booklet in the series.

Steven C. Mathews is an educator who has spent over 30 years in educational publishing, including stints as managing editor of education for the College Division of Allyn & Bacon and as editor in chief of PRO-ED. He served two terms as president of the Austin, Texas, Chapter of the Council for Exceptional Children and has served on advisory committees for the American Speech-Language-Hearing Association, Council for Learning Disabilities, and Texas Council for Exceptional Children. His publications include tests and therapy materials.

It has been my privilege to work closely with both Saul and Steve. I participated with Saul in several of his first research publications and coauthored with him my most recent publication. I know firsthand that he is an excellent researcher, teacher, and author. I know of no one better qualified to produce this series. I have also worked closely with Steve, who served as managing editor for a number of my publications, including my own *How To Manage Behavior Series*. His skill in guiding the selection of topics and in shaping and polishing manuscripts is unparalleled in my experience. Their cooperative efforts make this series a valuable contribution to the field of teacher education.

R. Vance Hall
Professor Emeritus
University of Kansas

PREFACE TO SERIES

The idea for the *How To Improve Classroom Behavior Series* grew from our conversations with R. Vance Hall. His popular series of booklets called *How To Manage Behavior* presents, in a step-by-step manner, behavioral procedures and techniques. Although they are practical and quick to read, the booklets in his series do not easily show a teacher who may be unfamiliar with behavioral techniques which ones would be best to use in specific situations. We agreed that a new series was needed—a series that would present behavioral techniques in booklets that each address a specific problem behavior that teachers encounter in their classrooms.

Development of the Series

We first wanted to determine what common behavior problems occur in the classroom. In reviewing the literature (Bender, 1987; Bibou-Nakou, Kiosseoglou, & Stogiannidou, 2000; Bickerstaff, Leon, & Hudson, 1997; Elam, 1987, 1989; Elam, Rose, & Gallup, 1994; Fagen, 1986; Gibbons & Jones, 1994; Greenlee & Ogletree, 1993; Jones, Quah, & Charlton, 1996; Malone, Bonitz, & Rickett, 1998; Mastrilli & Brown, 1999; Ordover, 1997), we found that common classroom behavior problems were consistently reported regardless of the age of the student, the type of classroom, the special needs of the student, the experience of the teacher, the passage of time, or the part of the world. This review produced a preliminary list of possible topics for the series.

The preliminary list was then compared to topics presented in textbooks used in courses on behavior management and classroom discipline (e.g., Charles, 1999; Kaplan, 1995, 2000; Sloane, 1988; Walker & Walker, 1991; Workman & Katz, 1995). The list was also evaluated by educators and psychologists from university and other school settings. Their input helped us create a revised list of topics.

The final list of topics, reflected in the titles of the *How To Improve Classroom Behavior Series*, was created by combining topics that had common themes and eliminating topics that did not lend themselves to the format of the series. After the final list was completed, we contacted potential authors for each booklet. Each author selected has a background related to the topic, knowledge of current behavioral principles, and experience working directly with teachers and students.

Format of the Series

All the booklets in the series were written in the same format. Each booklet includes the following:

- Practical and nontechnical information
- All the information a teacher needs to implement a strategy
- Step-by-step strategy presentation
- Numerous strategy suggestions from which the reader can choose
- Numerous examples of various levels of problem severity, ages of students, and instructional settings
- Interactive learning procedures with space and prompts for the reader to make oral or written responses
- References and suggestions for further readings

Uses of the Series

Each of the booklets in the series may be used independently or in conjunction with the other booklets. Each can be read and the information used by regular classroom teachers, special education teachers, teachers in collaborative classrooms, school psychologists, and anyone else who has students who exhibit the behavior that is the topic of the booklet.

The design of the booklets allows them to be used without additional information. However, they also lend themselves to workshop, in-service, or consultation situations. They are ideal for a special education teacher, school psychologist, or other consultant to share with a teacher who requests information or who reports a problem in her or his classroom.

Acknowledgments

We would first like to thank our friend R. Vance Hall for his advice, counsel, and patience, and for his writing the foreword to the series. The series would not exist without Vance's contributions.

We would also like to thank the contributors to the series. They all have prepared manuscripts following a prescribed format in a very short period of time. The many people at PRO-ED who have contributed to the series from its inception through its publication also have earned our thanks and respect.

Saul Axelrod and
Steven C. Mathews
Series Editors

Series References

Bender, W. N. (1987). Correlates of classroom behavior problems among learning disabled and nondisabled children in mainstream classes. *Learning Disabilities Quarterly, 10,* 317–324.

Bibou-Nakou, I., Kiosseoglou, G., & Stogiannidou, A. (2000). Elementary teacher's perceptions regarding school behavior problems: Implications for school psychological services. *Psychology in the Schools, 37,* 123–134.

Bickerstaff, S., Leon, S. H., & Hudson, J. G. (1997). Preserving the opportunity for education: Texas' alternative education programs for disruptive youth. *Journal of Law and Education, 26,* 1–39.

Charles, C. M. (1999). *Building classroom discipline* (6th ed.). New York: Longman.

Elam, S. M. (1987). Differences between educators and the public on questions of education policy. *Phi Delta Kappan, 69,* 294–296.

Elam, S. M. (1989). The second Gallup/Phi Delta Kappa poll of teachers' attitudes toward the public schools. *Phi Delta Kappan, 70,* 785–798.

Elam, S. M., Rose, L. C., & Gallup, A. M. (1994). The 26th annual Phi Delta Kappa/Gallup poll of the public's attitude toward the public schools. *Phi Delta Kappan, 76,* 41–56.

Fagen, S. A. (1986). Least intensive interventions for classroom behavior problems. *Pointer, 31,* 21–28.

Gibbons, L., & Jones, L. (1994). Novice teachers' reflectivity upon their classroom management. (ERIC Documentation Reproduction Service No. ED386446)

Greenlee, A. R., & Ogletree, E. J. (1993). Teachers' attitude toward student discipline problems and classroom management strategies. (ERIC Documentation Reproduction Service No. ED364330)

Jones, K., Quah, M. L., & Charlton, T. (1996). Behaviour which primary and special school teachers in Singapore find most troublesome. *Research in Education, 55,* 62–73.

Kaplan, J. S. (1995). *Beyond behavior modification: A cognitive–behavioral approach to behavior management in the school* (3rd ed.). Austin, TX: PRO-ED.

Kaplan, J. S. (2000). *Beyond functional assessment: A social–cognitive approach to the evaluation of behavior problems in children and youth.* Austin, TX: PRO-ED.

Malone, B. G., Bonitz, D. A., & Rickett, M. M. (1998). Teacher perceptions of disruptive behavior: Maintaining instructional focus. *Educational Horizons, 76,* 189–194.

Mastrilli, T. M., & Brown, D. S. (1999). Elementary student teachers' cases: An analysis of dilemmas and solutions. *Action in Teacher Education, 21,* 50–60.

Ordover, E. (1997). *Inclusion of students with disabilities who are labeled "disruptive": Issues papers for legal advocates and parents.* Boston: Center for Law and Education.

Sloane, H. N. (1988). *The good kid book: How to solve the 16 most common behavior problems.* Champaign, IL: Research Press.

Walker, H. M., & Walker, J. E. (1991). *Coping with noncompliance in the classroom: A positive approach for teachers.* Austin, TX: PRO-ED.

Workman, E. A., & Katz, A. M. (1995). *Teaching behavioral self-control to students* (2nd ed.). Austin, TX: PRO-ED.

How To Improve Classroom Behavior Series

How To Help Students Remain Seated

How To Deal Effectively with Lying, Stealing, and Cheating

How To Prevent and Safely Manage Physical Aggression and Property Destruction

How To Help Students Complete Classwork and Homework Assignments

How To Help Students Play and Work Together

How To Deal with Students Who Challenge and Defy Authority

How To Deal Effectively with Whining and Tantrum Behaviors

How To Help Students Follow Directions, Pay Attention, and Stay on Task

Introduction

If you cannot keep your students in their seats, you have no chance of achieving classroom control. Frequently, teachers tell me that they have several problems going on simultaneously and wonder which one to target first for modification. Invariably, I recommend out-of-seat behavior (if it is on the teacher's list). When students are out of their seats, there is no end to the trouble they can get into. They can go to another part of the classroom to speak to a classmate. They can poke another student in the back. They can damage classroom property.

Of course, there are good reasons for students to be out of their seats. But the behavior should be under the control of the teacher not at the whim of the student. A student can get up to sharpen a pencil, work on the computer, or use the restroom. But these actions should only be engaged in with the permission of the teacher or when they conform to classroom rules. In this way, the teacher can regulate the number of children who are out of their seats and for how long, and obtain classroom control.

The problem of out-of-seat behavior has been around for as long as there have been schools. Yet there are steps a teacher can take to reduce this problem without too much difficulty. This book focuses on a set of steps that can be applied to out-of-seat behavior as well as to other classroom management problems.

Steps for Modifying Behavior

1. Choose a Behavior To Modify

In this case the choice is simple. Out-of-seat behavior is the behavior to modify. If other behaviors are a problem, they can be dealt with later. Meanwhile, when out-of-seat behavior is reduced, other problems sometimes also diminish, or disappear, and student productivity sometimes increases.

2. Define the Behavior

It is important to clearly define the behavior of concern. A careful definition allows a student to know exactly what is permissible and what is not. A clear definition is a good communication device between a teacher and a student. A good definition has certain characteristics. First, it refers to *observable behavior*—a behavior that a teacher can see rather than infer. Second, a good definition is *precise*. The behavior is so clearly defined that there can be no doubt as to whether it occurred. Third, a well-defined behavior is *inclusive*. It includes all instances of the behavior and is easily distinguished from noninstances of the behavior.

Consider the following definition of out-of-seat behavior: any instance in which a student's buttocks lose contact with the bottom of her or his seat. The definition refers to observable behavior. A teacher can see when it happens. The definition is precise. There is usually no doubt as to whether a student's buttocks lose contact with the seat. But the definition may not be inclusive. What if a student propels himself along the room with a chair attached to his rear end? Thus, it is important for a teacher to observe a behavior over several sessions and note exactly what she means by a particular behavior. Different teachers can define out-of-seat behavior differently and all be correct. Definitions are idiosyncratic to a teacher's situation.

Question 1

What are the characteristics of a well-defined behavior? Give a definition of out-of-seat behavior that meets these characteristics.

3. Functionally Assess the Behavior

Students perform a behavior for a reason. Another way of saying this is that behavior serves a function. Functional assessment procedures help determine why a person performs a certain behavior. This is valuable because identifying the function a behavior serves can help to devise more effective intervention plans. Consider out-of-seat behavior. A student may perform the behavior because of the attention a teacher gives her, because she wishes to avoid an unpleasant assignment, or because she has access to a favorite item when she leaves her seat. Each possible function calls for a different intervention strategy. If the function is to get attention, the teacher could give the student attention if she remains seated for a period of time. If the student leaves her seat to avoid an undesirable task, the teacher could give her a break each time she does a small portion of the assignment. If she leaves her seat to attain a desired item, the teacher could give her access to the item after remaining seated for a specified period of time. Procedures for precisely identifying the function of a behavior are very sophisticated and exceed the resources available in most classrooms. Nevertheless, a teacher's best hypothesis as to the function of a behavior is usually valuable in selecting an intervention.

Question 2

What is the purpose of a functional assessment? Name three possible functions of a behavior.

4. Take a Baseline on the Behavior

Before intervening on a behavior, it is necessary to determine how often it is presently occurring. Thus, it is important to measure the behavior under normal or *baseline* conditions. Usually, 5 days is sufficient to establish a baseline. By establishing a baseline, a teacher can later judge whether a procedure is working. One way of establishing a baseline is to count the number of out-of-seat behaviors occurring each day. Another way is to have a timer sound periodically and note whether the behavior is occurring. Then a teacher would have a record of the frequency or percentage of time out-of-seat behavior is occurring.

Question 3

> What is baseline? Indicate two measures a teacher can use to assess baseline.

a. _____

b. _____

5. Intervene on the Behavior

A later section of this book will be devoted to the specific interventions a teacher can use to modify out-of-seat behavior. Meanwhile, a good intervention is inexpensive and easy to apply. It is also helpful to be aware of what other teachers have found to be effective. A procedure that works with some students has a good chance of being effective with other students. To a large extent, the intervention will depend on the teacher's judgment as to what is likely to be effective, what will be compatible with a smooth classroom routine, what will be comfortable for the teacher, and what will be socially acceptable to administration and parents. During the intervention period, the teacher should continue to collect data on out-of-seat behavior. It is critical that the teacher apply a procedure consistently during the intervention period. Otherwise, it is impossible to tell whether the procedure was ineffective or whether it was applied improperly.

Question 4

What are the characteristics of an appropriate intervention?

_____

_____

_____

_____

_____

_____

_____

6. Graph and Evaluate the Outcome

Collecting baseline and intervention data and storing them in a drawer does the teacher no good. It is necessary to graph the data on a daily basis (see Figures 1 and 2). Examination of the graph serves some important purposes. The main purpose is to let the teacher know whether the procedures are working. When the procedures are working, the teacher can continue to use them. If they are not working, it is time to look for an alternative.

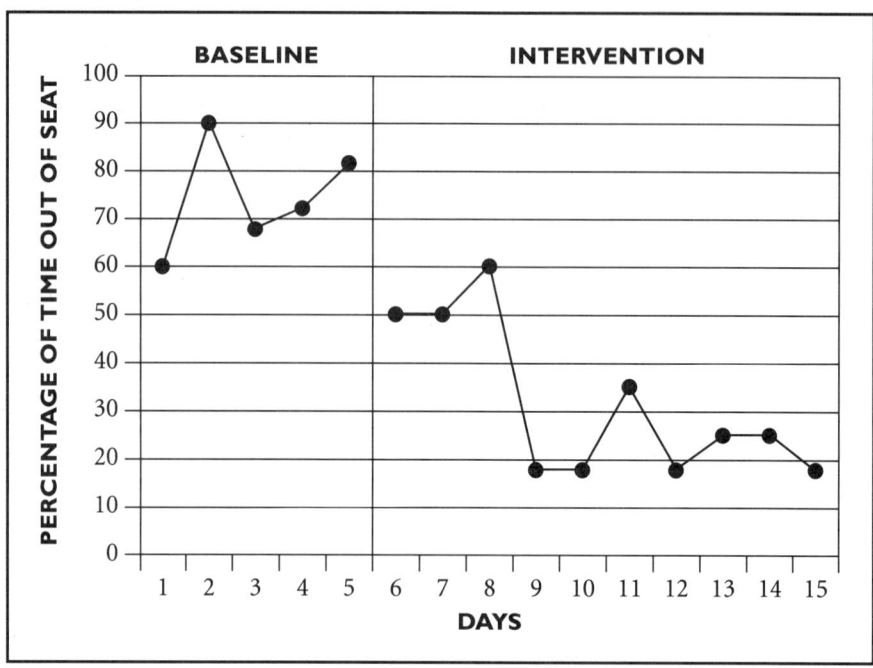

Figure 1. The percentage of time out of seat.

Also a graph showing substantial improvement will reinforce the efforts of teachers and students and will allow more effective communications with other educators and parents. Figure 1 indicates that the intervention is working; Figure 2 reveals a procedure that is ineffective.

Question 5

Why is it important to collect and graph data on out-of-seat behavior?

_____
_____
_____
_____

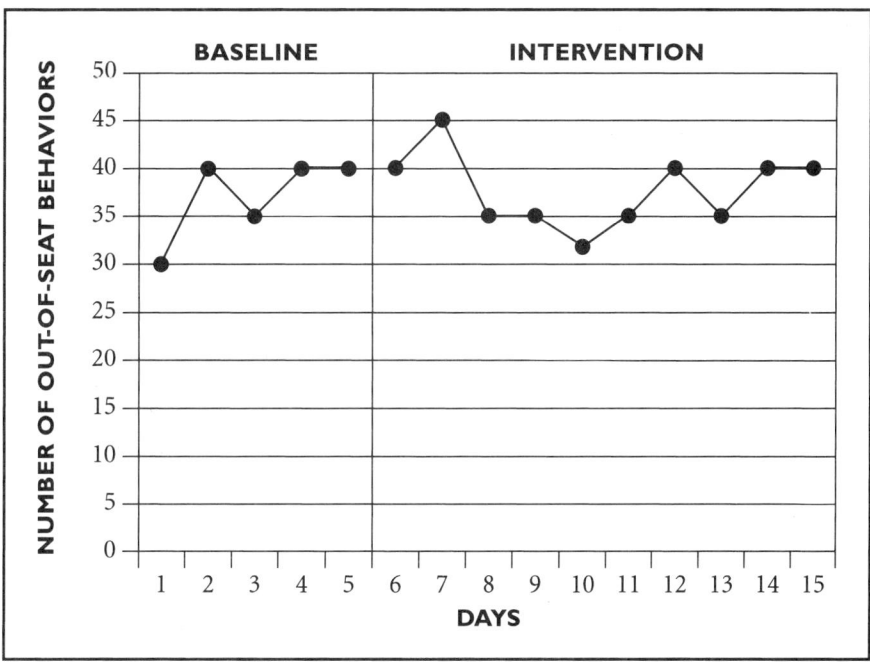

Figure 2. The number of out-of-seat behaviors.

7. Revise the Program if Necessary

Success is never guaranteed when a teacher intervenes on a problem such as out-of-seat behavior. No matter how effective a procedure has been in other situations, there is no certainty that it will work in the present case. Thus, teachers must be prepared to revise their interventions when the results are unsatisfactory. Sometimes this means making a small adjustment in the intervention, such as when a procedure is showing some effectiveness but the teacher desires further improvements in the behavior or when a procedure is effective but inconvenient or expensive. At other times it is necessary to abandon a procedure entirely and devise another one. Teachers frequently ask me how patient they should be before giving up on a procedure. My experience has been that if an intervention is not effective after a week or two of appropriate application, it is probably time to look for an alternative.

Question 6

> When is it necessary to revise an intervention?

_____

_____

_____

As shown on the flow chart (see Figure 3), when a procedure is effective, a teacher should continue using it and enjoy the outcome. When a procedure does not work, it is necessary to devise an alternative intervention. Thus, the system is self-correcting. A teacher keeps working on an intervention until he or she finds one that works.

Question 7

> On a separate sheet of paper, describe a flow chart depicting each of the steps in modifying behavior.

Importance of Being Positive

The best way to modify behavior is through positive reinforcement procedures. In a *positive reinforcement* procedure, a person performs a

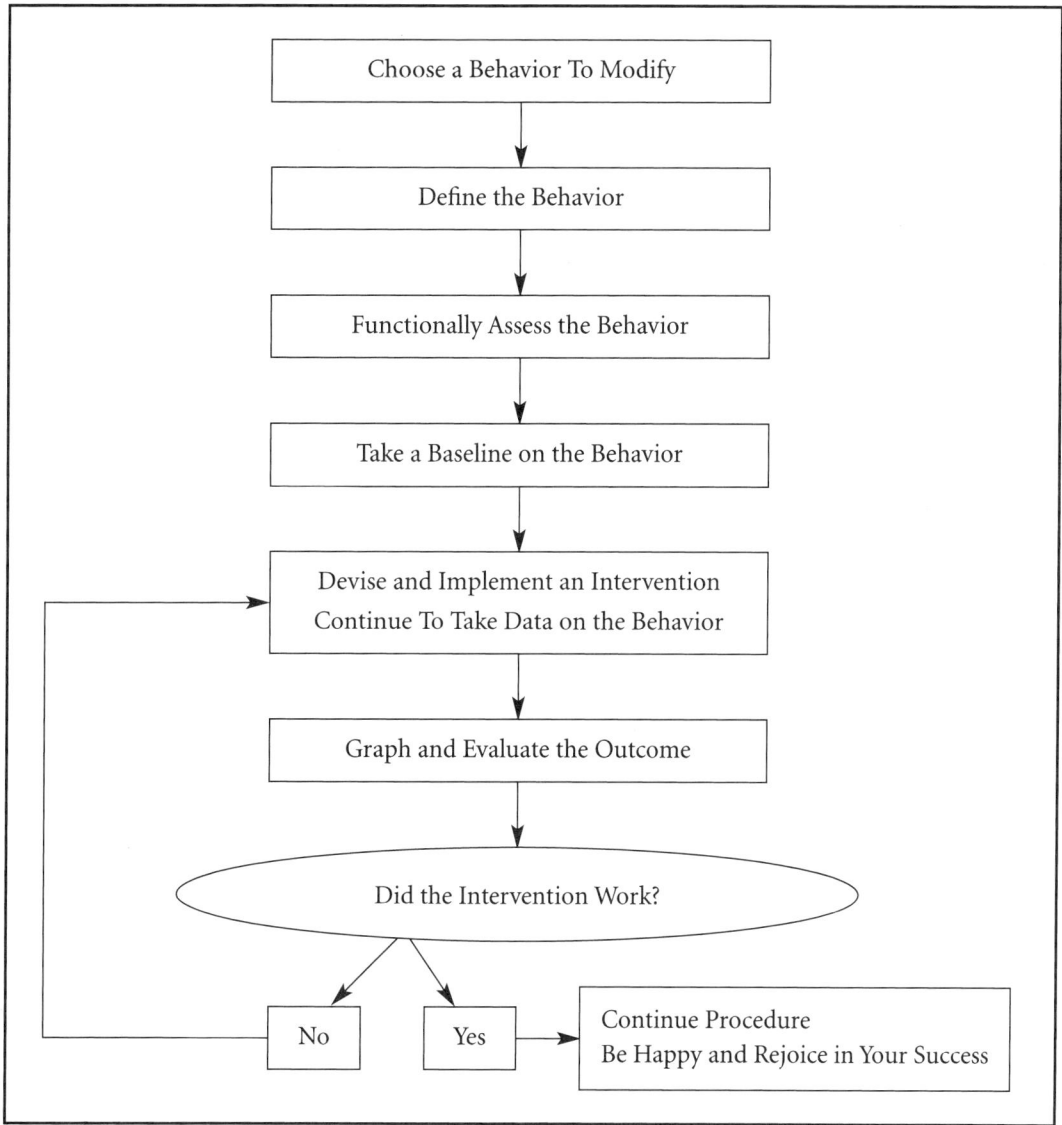

Figure 3. A flow chart representing the steps in modifying inappropriate behaviors.

behavior and experiences a pleasant consequence. If the behavior occurs more frequently than it did in the past, positive reinforcement has occurred. Suppose, for example, that the teacher compliments a student after she asks permission to leave her seat. If the student asks permission more frequently than she did in the past, positive reinforcement has occurred and the compliment is a *positive reinforcer.* Suppose, on the other hand, that the teacher periodically gives a class extra free time when all students are in their seats. If the rate of in-seat behavior stays the same or goes down, we cannot say that positive reinforcement has occurred.

Question 8

> How can a teacher determine whether something is a positive reinforcer?

_____

_____

_____

_____

Teachers should try to use positive reinforcement procedures whenever possible. Unfortunately, this is often not the case. Frequently, teachers try to change behavior through detentions, unpleasant notes to parents, and suspensions. Even when these techniques work—and they often do not—they create an unpleasant classroom atmosphere that both students and teachers dislike. Although I believe that punishment procedures are sometimes helpful, and I suggest one or two later in the book, most of the time teachers should use positive reinforcement procedures. Even when punishment is used for inappropriate behavior, it should be combined with copious positive reinforcement for appropriate behavior (e.g., lots of praise). This will make the intervention more effective and create a happier classroom environment.

Positive reinforcement procedures work and create win–win situations. Students like being in a classroom in which behavior is based on positive reinforcement procedures. They brighten when their behaviors are positively reinforced. Teachers enjoy teaching with positive reinforcement procedures because the process is so gratifying. It is fun for a teacher to walk into a classroom in which he or she is using positive reinforcement. It is not fun to walk into a classroom in which the teacher is continually reprimanding student behavior and the teacher and students may trade insults and threats. When teachers use positive reinforcement procedures and student behavior improves, a warm, caring relationship often develops between the teacher and students.

Positive reinforcers fall into three categories—social, activity, and tangible. Each has its place in classroom management. On a moment-to-moment basis, however, teachers should use social reinforcers such as praise for students who are sitting in their seats and working hard. Teachers can use activity reinforcers such as extra free time if students remain in their seats for a stated period of time. Tangible reinforcers, such as a grab from a grab bag, can be used periodically for exceptional performance. Given that student preferences for reinforcers vary, a teacher should not assume that some event is a reinforcer. Rather, the behavior of a student will reveal whether something is a reinforcer. The question is how can the teacher identify potential positive reinforcers for a student or a group of students?

One procedure for identifying *potential* positive reinforcers is to present two or more potential reinforcers and have a student choose one of them. After 10 or 15 trials, one or two of the choices tends to dominate and reveals a likely reinforcer for a student.

A second procedure is to ask a student or a group to list and rank potential reinforcers. This process requires patience because students sometimes request prohibitively expensive reinforcers such as a trip to Disneyworld. With teacher perseverance students can usually be induced to make reasonable requests.

A third procedure for identifying potential positive reinforcers is to note what a student spends a lot of time doing. A student who spends most free time on a computer or shooting baskets is indicating that such activities are probably reinforcers for his or her behavior. Sometimes students engage in activities that are inappropriate at the time they are occurring. At other times, however, these activities might be used as reinforcers. For example, teachers do not want students to read a hidden comic book in the middle of a social studies lesson or to talk to classmates on the other side of the classroom. But reading the comic book or talking to a classmate for 5 minutes might be used as reinforcers at other times of the day.

Finally, it is helpful to note which events follow an undesirable behavior. Thus, a preschooler might be picked up and comforted by a teacher following crying incidents. Such teacher actions likely are reinforcing the crying behavior. Instead, the teacher can give such attention to a student following a period of appropriate behavior. A high school teacher might find that he is giving a student a lot of attention, in the form of reprimands, each time he leaves his seat. The teacher might then give the student attention, in the form of praise, while he is in his seat and working.

Question 9

Describe three ways in which a teacher can identify a potential positive reinforcer.

a. _____

_____

b. _____

_____

c. _____

_____

A point I wish to emphasize is that the procedures listed for identifying positive reinforcers are merely suggestive. They are not definitive. That is, the procedures *might* lead to the identification of reinforcers. The only way to determine whether something is a positive reinforcer is to have it follow a behavior and see whether it increases the rate of the behavior. If it increases the behavior, it is positive reinforcer. If it does not increase the rate of the behavior, it is not a reinforcer, even if a student expresses an interest in and enthusiasm for the activity.

How To Help Students Remain Seated   13

Question 10

What is wrong with claiming in advance that a particular event is a positive reinforcer for a student?

_____
_____
_____
_____
_____
_____
_____

In Table 1, I have provided a list of potential reinforcers according to the type of reinforcer—social, activity, or tangible. The reinforcers are also divided according to early grades and later grades. The list is under constant revision based mainly on the recommendations of my students, who are mostly preservice and in-service teachers.

Question 11

Identify five social, activity, and tangible events that can serve as potential reinforcers. Do not use any examples given in this book.

Social   a. _____

           b. _____

           c. _____

           d. _____

           e. _____

TABLE I
Classroom Reinforcers (Group and Individual)

	Social	Activity	Tangible
Early Childhood/ Elementary	Positive comments such as "Good work," "Thanks for being on time," "I like the way you waited," "Wonderful!" Pat on the back Complimentary note home to parents Outstanding students list High five Display of work Applause from classmates	Have extra art time Feed class pets Have backwards day Sit next to classmate of choice Help teacher run errands Have a party Have extra time on computer Play classroom game Have extra P.E. time Erase chalkboards Watch videotape or TV Eat lunch with teacher Be first in line Play with puzzles Help a classmate Have leisure reading Build model Listen to private radio Play with clay Help in library Collect lunch money	Pencils, pens, ribbons Stickers, stars, balloons Treasure chest of various items Crayons, erasers, puzzles Books, coloring books Magic markers, badges Colored chalk, comic books Silly putty, puzzles, yo-yo Fruit, popcorn Cereal, nuts Pretzels, raisins Juice
Junior/Senior High School	Smiles, winks, shakes hand Victory sign, thumbs up Pat on back Complimentary phone call to student or parents High achievement list Private compliment Honor roll Complimentary note Increase course grade	Have extra free time Play checkers, chess, or card games Listen to private radio or tape Have classroom party Have day with no homework Go on a field trip Have extra gym time Have extra lunch time Work on computer Teach another student Watch a videotape Have a class outside Observe a science demonstration Talk to another student	Posters Sports equipment Music tapes Magazines Blank tapes Paperback book Ticket to show Pizza, dried fruit Nuts, pretzels, chips Juice, soft drinks Demo CDs

Activity   a. _____

           b. _____

           c. _____

           d. _____

           e. _____

Tangible   a. _____

           b. _____

           c. _____

           d. _____

           e. _____

Procedures To Help Students Remain Seated

Here comes the fun part. In this section I describe the specific techniques that I have found particularly helpful for keeping students in their seats. The procedures have been successfully used for students at every grade level. They have also sometimes failed to work with students at various grade levels. There is no certainty that a procedure that works with some students will work with all students. Therefore, it is important for teachers to be able to conduct a variety of interventions and to make adjustments with each of the procedures when they do not attain desired results. Likewise, it is helpful to be aware of techniques that other teachers have found effective, because experience shows that a procedure that works with some students will often work with other students.

In a certain situation, it may be that one or two students exhibit out-of-seat behaviors at a high rate or that most of the students in the classroom frequently leave their seats. A teacher then must decide whether to use an *individual contingency* or a *group contingency*. In an individual contingency, a student earns reinforcers according to her own performance. In the type of group contingency described here, the behavior of all the students determines the amount of reinforcement the group receives.

Question 12

Distinguish between an individual and a group contingency.

___

___

___

___

___

1. Using DRL To Reduce Out-of-Seat Behaviors

Differential reinforcement of low rate of response (DRL) is a strong procedure for reducing out-of-seat behaviors. It works as follows: Suppose a class has an average of 50 out-of-seat behaviors during baseline. The teacher then specifies the upper limit on the number of out-of-seat behaviors a class can exhibit and still receive a reinforcer, such as having the teacher read a 10-minute story at the end of the morning. Because the baseline level is 50, 40 out-of-seat behaviors might be a reasonable goal. The teacher could then list the numbers 40, 39, 38, . . . 0 on the chalkboard. Each time a student leaves her seat without permission, the teacher crosses off the highest intact number. If any numbers remain at the end of the morning, *the students receive the entire 10-minute reinforcer.* For example, an outcome such as the following would lead to the 10-minute reinforcer:

How To Help Students Remain Seated   17

~~40~~, ~~30~~,...~~X~~, 6, 5, 4, 3, 2, 1, 0

The teacher might still feel that the rate of out-of-seat behaviors is too high a figure. He or she could then gradually lower the upper limit to 35, 30, and so on.

DRL can be set up as an individual or a group contingency. As an individual contingency, a student could be offered the opportunity to be classroom messenger at the end of the day if he or she had fewer than 10 out-of-seat behaviors. This procedure can be used at both the elementary and secondary levels. My students have provided some secondary education examples of interventions. In one case a secondary education mathematics teacher used a DRL procedure to reduce out-of-seat behaviors. The baseline was 20 per period. Each day that the class had fewer than 12 incidents, the students received a point. When the class achieved five points, the students had a day without a homework assignment. The procedure reduced the behaviors to less than half the baseline level. In another case a science teacher had an average of 15 out-of-seat behaviors per 35-minute class period. The teacher offered the students a short break at the end of class if the level of out-of-seat behaviors was below 10. Out-of-seat behaviors decreased to a third of the baseline level.

2. Using Response Cost To Reduce Out-of-Seat Behaviors

Using this procedure the teacher offers students extra free time or another reinforcer if they stay in their seats. He puts the numbers on the chalkboard as follows:

~~10~~, ~~9~~, ~~8~~, 7, 6, 5, 4, 3, 2, 1, 0

Each time a student leaves her seat, the teacher crosses off the highest intact number and the group loses 1 minute of its extra free time. In this example, there were three out-of-seat behaviors, so the group had 7 extra minutes of free time. The difference between DRL and response cost is that in DRL a person or group receives the entire reinforcer when the number of out-of-seat behaviors falls below the stated criterion. In the case of response cost, each out-of-seat behavior costs the person or group a portion of the reinforcer.

This is an amazingly powerful procedure. I have seen a class go from over 100 out-of-seat behaviors per hour to 1 per hour in less than a week. It is also a procedure that applies to secondary as well as elementary students. A secondary education teacher in one of my classes used response cost to reduce out-of-seat behaviors in her high school English class. She started the week with 45 points representing the number of minutes of her daily class. Each time a student left his seat without permission, the teacher crossed off the highest remaining number. On Friday the students had a party corresponding to the number of remaining points. If the students were out of their seats 15 times in a week, for example, they would have a 30-minute party on Friday. Out-of-seat behaviors deceased rapidly, and the students even got more work done in less time because the classroom was more orderly.

I would like to make two additional points about this procedure. First, the procedure just described is a group contingency. Response cost can also be used as an individual contingency in which one student loses a point for each out-of-seat behavior. Second, response cost is technically classified as a punishment procedure. Yet some of the objections to punishment are minimized in this example because the teacher is using extra free time not time normally due students. Also, positive reinforcement can be introduced by having the teacher lavishly praise the students for their increased in-seat behavior and by providing bonuses for outstanding performances.

Question 13

Distinguish between DRL and response cost.

3. Using DRO To Reduce Out-of-Seat Behaviors

Differential reinforcement of other behavior (DRO) is another effective procedure to deal with out-of-seat behavior. As with most other procedures, DRO can be done on an individual or group contingent basis. The present example involves a group contingency. A teacher might note that students leave their seats an average of once every 5 minutes. The teacher would then set a timer for 6 minutes and tell the students that they could earn one point if no one leaves her or his seat between the present time and the time that the timer goes off in 6 minutes. If 6 minutes go by without an out-of-seat behavior, the students would receive a point, and the teacher would reset the timer for another 6 minutes. If a student leaves his seat before the timer goes off, the teacher would point out the infraction and reset the timer for another 6 minutes. At the end of the session the students exchange their accumulated points for an agreed-upon privilege (e.g., time to talk to each other quietly). As student behavior improves, the teacher can gradually increase the length of the intervals to 8 minutes, 10 minutes, and so forth.

A problem that may occur with DRO is that students may become disruptive right after receiving the reinforcer. After all, for students the best time to leave their seats is right after the timer goes off and they receive a point. To correct this problem the teacher can make use of two DRO intervals. There can be a shorter interval (e.g., 6 minutes) following a period of no out-of-seat behaviors. There can be a longer interval (e.g., 10 minutes) following an out-of-seat behavior. This will often be an effective disincentive for out-of-seat behaviors immediately following reception of a reinforcer.

4. Using Unpredictable Timings To Catch In-Seat Behavior

Using this procedure the teacher informs his students that he wants them to stay in their seats unless they have permission to leave. He sets a timer to go off at an instant that students cannot predict. For example, if class begins at 8:45, the timer might go off at 9:02. Next it might go off at 9:35, and then at 9:37, and so forth. Each instance the timer rings, the teacher checks to see if all students are in their seats. If students are all in their seats, they receive a point toward some event such as a classroom party, which requires a stated number of points. The next day the teacher sets the timer to go off in a different sequence of times.

Certain conditions must be in effect for this procedure to work. First, students must not be able to predict when the timer will go off. The teacher should vary the sequence within and among days. Second, students should not be able to see the position of the timer, or they may beat the system by being in their seats just before the timer sounds but not at other times. Finally, the teacher needs to set some short intervals, lest students learn that the timer will not ring shortly following the previous instance.

Question 14

Distinguish between DRO and unpredictable timings.

5. Using the "Good Behavior" Game To Reduce Out-of-Seat Behaviors

This is a procedure that students and teachers usually like. The teacher breaks the classroom into two teams, often one side of the classroom versus the other. The teacher informs the students that they can leave their seats only when they obtain permission. Each time a student breaks this rule, a point is put under the team's name, for example:

Owls	Wildcats
///	////

The team with the fewer points is the winner and receives extra privileges, such as putting students' names on a winner's chart, lining up first for lunch, or wearing smiley-face badges. If both teams score below a stated criterion (e.g., five), both teams can be winners. If the same team keeps winning, it may be necessary for some students to change teams to make the scores more nearly equal. If one or two students make it impossible for their team to win, it may be necessary to take them out of the game and place them on individual contingencies.

A variation of this technique is to combine the good behavior game with the procedure of using unpredictable timings. When the timer goes off and all students from one team are in their seats, the team gets a point. At the end of a session, the team with the greater number of points is the winner.

6. Beating a Previous Best Score To Decrease Out-of-Seat Behaviors

This procedure is a lot of fun and it often works well. The teacher keeps track of how many times a group of students leave their seats during baseline. Let's say baseline averages 82 times per day. This figure is presented on the chalkboard or on a flip chart. The goal for the students is to beat their best score each following day. When the students achieve a new best score, it is highlighted (e.g., in bold or red) as follows:

82 77 63 66 **52** 52 **39** ...

Sometimes this procedure provides sufficient motivation for students to improve their behavior. At other times, it is necessary to provide an additional reinforcer (e.g., extra time to watch a video). In such cases, having a lower limit that does not need to be bettered for reinforcement to be delivered may be helpful. For example, any time the total is 15 or below, the teacher could provide a reinforcer, even if the score is not a new best. This helps to guarantee that appropriate behavior is reinforced.

7. Using Daily Report Cards To Decrease Out-of-Seat Behaviors

This is an easy procedure for the teacher and it is often highly effective. Let's consider an example with one student, although the procedure can be applied to several students or even an entire class. Suppose a student is averaging 20 out-of-seat behaviors per day during baseline. During intervention the teacher keeps track of these behaviors and sends a report home to the parents with the total for the day. If the student reaches a criterion of 15 or fewer out-of-seat behaviors, the student receives a privilege at home. The privilege can be the opportunity to stay up late, an increase in allowance, or points toward the right to have a friend sleep over on the weekend. As the student's behavior improves, the criterion for reinforcement can be gradually lowered.

The advantages of this procedure are that it is cost-free to the teacher; it allows for the awarding of more powerful reinforcers than are sometimes available in school; it avoids the problem of giving only some students in-class rewards; and it improves communications between home and school.

If teachers use the daily report-card procedure, it is imperative that they stress with parents the positive reinforcement nature of the program. The purpose of the program is to provide home-based reinforcers when a student's behavior improves. *The daily report-card procedure should not be used as a vehicle for punishing misbehavior.* Teachers should also be aware that some parents will not conduct the program according to the rules. Some parents will neglect to deliver earned reinforcers, and other parents will give out rewards even when their child does not earn them if the child promises, "I will do better next week." Therefore, a teacher should only use the daily report-card procedure when there is good reason to believe that parents will carry it out properly.

Question 15

Discuss the advantages and disadvantages of the daily report-card procedure.

8. Using a Response-Cost Lottery To Decrease Out-of-Seat Behaviors

This procedure combines the advantages of response cost and an element of the unknown to make it exciting. Students start the day with, let's say, five slips of paper on which they write their names. Each time a student leaves her seat without permission, she loses one of the slips. At the end of the day, the teacher collects all the remaining slips and puts them in a container, which she shakes. Three slips are randomly chosen. The students who are chosen get a privilege such as a grab from a box of items purchased from a dollar store. Obviously, the fewer out-of-seat behaviors a student performs, the more slips of paper she retains and the greater the chance she has of receiving the reward. If some students consistently retain their slips but are seldom picked, the teacher should increase the number of slips that are chosen daily.

Pointers for Successfully Modifying Behavior

Some teachers are very successful at modifying out-of-seat and other behaviors. Other teachers are less successful. What are the successful teachers doing differently? Sometimes the differences are major; sometimes the differences are subtle. Obviously, small changes in the manner in which a teacher conducts a program can sometimes make a major difference in the outcome. The purpose of this section is to suggest some actions a teacher can take to increase the likelihood that her efforts will be successful in a reasonable period of time.

1. Make Frequent Adjustments in Your Procedures

This is where the action is. Sometimes I will describe a procedure to my students (future or in-service teachers) and someone will ask whether it is okay to apply the procedure in a somewhat different manner. It is at these times that I realize that I have not done my job properly. *Teachers should always exercise their best judgment when applying an intervention.* Teachers know their students' behaviors better than anyone else in the school. They should use this knowledge to adjust the procedures they are applying to their students' behavior. Some adjustments a teacher can make are as follows:

   a. Teachers might check behaviors more frequently (e.g., on an average of every 10 minutes rather than an average of every 20 minutes).

   b. Teachers might give out reinforcers more frequently (e.g., twice a day rather than once a day).

c. Sometimes a reinforcer that was once effective becomes less effective. In these cases teachers can change reinforcers or use a variety of reinforcers.

d. Teachers sometimes find that making a change in the physical environment improves the effectiveness of an intervention. This might involve moving two students away from each other, arranging desks in a different configuration, and so forth.

e. Teachers can seek the recommendations of their students as to how to make an intervention more effective. Some evidence suggests that when students participate in determining the terms of their programs, the programs are more effective.

Question 16

Name three adjustments not described in this book that a teacher can take to make a procedure more effective.

a. _____

b. _____

c. _____

2. Prioritize and Work with Only One or Two Behaviors at a Time

Sometimes teachers face situations in which there are several behavior problems occurring at one time. Students might be out of their seats, talking out, teasing each other, and disturbing each other's property. Some teachers, understandably, wish to reduce the occurrence of each of these behaviors simultaneously. The problem is that this approach often fails because it requires too much behavior change. It is better to select one or two behaviors, get them under control, and then work on the remaining behaviors. The question then becomes which behavior a teacher should choose to modify, given that there are several problems. The choice is the teacher's, but should be made according to which behavior change would result in the greatest payoff. This is usually out-of-seat behavior for reasons stated earlier.

Question 17

What are four behavior problems you have or are likely to encounter in the classroom? Prioritize them in the order of importance for behavior change.

a. _____

b. _____

c. _____

d. _____

3. Require Only a Gradual Improvement in Behavior

There is a general rule that teachers should follow: *If a student's behavior improves, her behavior should be reinforced.* I have seen many situations in which a student's behavior markedly improves, yet does not meet the criterion for reinforcement. In such cases a student's behavior is likely to deteriorate. Thus, if a class has averaged 20 out-of-seat behaviors per hour during baseline, the criterion for reinforcement might be 17 or fewer misbehaviors during the initial stage of intervention. If a student is typically out of her seat an average of every 10 minutes, the criterion might be 12 consecutive minutes of in-seat behavior in order to receive a selected reinforcer. In both cases, however, when improvement occurs and is sustained for a few days, the criterion for reinforcement should be gradually be made more stringent. In the latter case, the criterion for reinforcement can go from 12 minutes, to 15 minutes, to 18 minutes, and so forth. Once an improvement in behavior has been achieved, future gains are likely.

Question 18

Describe or hypothesize a situation in which out-of-seat behavior is a problem. Describe a procedure that might modify the behavior. Indicate how you would set the original criterion for reinforcement and how you might later change it.

4. Use Procedures that Are Easily Implemented and Inexpensive

Unfortunately, people have devised many behavioral procedures that are very effective, but are discarded by teachers because they are too difficult or expensive to implement. At times this has occurred because researchers working with teachers had the benefit of generous research grants that supported extra personnel and costly reinforcers. When the grant expired and the researchers were gone, the teacher stopped using the effective program because it was unreasonable to maintain with the usual classroom resources.

It is imperative that teachers use only those interventions that are easy to implement and do not strain the budget. Both of these conditions can be met. Some of the most useful procedures I have encountered were devised by in-service teachers enrolled in a classroom management course I taught. They were required to carry out a classroom management study in their classrooms and had only themselves and a small budget to implement the program. Many of the procedures amazed me with their creativity and usefulness. In addition, effective teachers continually search for ways to simplify their interventions. With respect to cost, many of the reinforcers listed earlier are free or inexpensive. (Check out the dollar stores when you get a chance.)

5. Organize All Aspects of the Program

This piece of advice might sound like something out of a Girl Scout or Boy Scout manual, but it is important. Behavioral programs should be conducted as smoothly as possible. Teachers should have data sheets readily available, rather than fumble through desk drawers when data sheets are needed. If a teacher is using a number chart for a response cost or DRL procedure, the numbers should be on the chalkboard before the students come into class. Reinforcers should be available as soon as they are earned. Data should be graphed daily, not weekly or less frequently. As teachers we frequently note that students who are doing poorly have messy desks, lose homework assignments, and have no quiet time or place to study at home. Yet we are not always aware of how organizational issues affect our ability to teach effectively.

6. Use Immediate Reinforcers Whenever Possible

Behavioral programs sometimes fail because there is a long delay between the time a student performs an appropriate behavior and a teacher delivers a reinforcer. It is important to note that new or improved behavior is weak behavior. If the behavior is not quickly and frequently followed by reinforcement, it is likely to disappear. If students must wait until the end of the day to receive a reinforcer, an otherwise well-constructed program may fail. In one case, I was working with a girl who was school phobic. The pleas of her parents to go to school were ignored. We devised a program in which the girl would receive a major reinforcer for attending the last 15 minutes of a school day. When the program was successful, we increased the requirement to 30 minutes and then to 45 minutes. Within a few weeks the girl asked that she be allowed to attend school for the entire day. (The teacher also programmed many small reinforcers throughout the day.)

The requirement that reinforcers be delivered immediately mainly applies to the early stages of learning. When behavior has improved and stabilized, it is often possible to delay reinforcement and still maintain effectiveness. In one case we used a DRL procedure four different times during a school day to reduce out-of-seat behaviors. The students could earn extra minutes of free time before the morning recess, before lunch, during the afternoon recess, and at the end of the school day. When the behavior was greatly reduced, we eliminated the extra free time during both of the recesses and later for lunch. At the end of the program, the only available free time was at the end of the day. Behavior can be maintained through delayed reinforcement procedures, but only after improvement is established and sustained through more immediate reinforcement.

7. Precisely Describe and Publicly Post the Rules

When students experience a new program, they are being asked to change their behavior in response to a set of rules that they have probably not experienced before. If the purpose of the program is to increase in-seat behavior, the students might wonder what happens when they leave their seats without permission to pick up a pencil they just dropped. What if they move their desk along the floor? Is that an out-of-seat behavior? It is important that teachers specify as many of the rules in advance as possible. Nevertheless, no one can be asked to predict all of the possible behaviors that will occur after a program is implemented. It is sometimes necessary to adapt the rules after a program is running. This should only be done, however, after the students are informed of the rule changes and are provided an explanation for the changes.

Whatever rules are devised for out-of-seat or other behaviors should not only be made clear, but also publicly posted. (In cases where students lack reading skills, icons can be used.) Teachers can then refer to the rules as class begins and students will have an opportunity to familiarize themselves with the rules throughout the class period.

8. Use Cues To Increase the Likelihood of Appropriate Behavior

Let us return to the point that new behavior is weak behavior. A crucial goal of behavioral teaching methods, whether the problem is classroom management or academic, is to train the behavior to fluency. This means that the behavior occurs immediately and correctly. It is automatic.

Yet such a goal cannot be achieved instantly. It takes assistance and practice. One way to assist students in the learning process is to give them as many cues as possible as to what they are expected to do. Teachers can remind students of the program as soon as they walk into class. Teachers can review the rules of the program frequently. They can point to charts referring to the program to cue appropriate behavior. As is true for the practice of immediately delivering reinforcers, the necessity to use these cues is most important at the start of a program. As student behavior improves and approaches fluency, the cues that prompt behavior can be gradually removed in a process known as *fading*.

Question 19

Describe a program for decreasing out-of-seat behavior and the cues you would provide to increase the likelihood that students will perform the behavior successfully.

9. Model the Desired Behavior

Speaking of cues to prompt appropriate behavior, perhaps the best way to achieve this is for the teacher to model the desired behavior. For most students modeling a behavior such as raising one's hand to get permission to leave the seat is no problem. Most students already have this skill. For students with severe handicaps or with very young children, however, there may be a skill deficit that can be remedied with a modeling program. In such cases, the teacher models the behaviors of raising her hand and asking permission to leave the seat. The teacher then prompts the student to imitate the behaviors. Initially, the teacher reinforces any attempt to imitate the behavior. Later, only closer approximations to the desired behavior are reinforced, until the behavior is occurring fluently.

Question 20

> Describe a sequence of steps for teaching a student to imitate the behavior of asking for permission to leave his or her seat.

10. Pair Social Reinforcers with Tangible or Activity Reinforcers

Sometimes teachers see tangible and activity reinforcers as unnatural. They are willing to use such reinforcers for a limited period of time and then wish to achieve classroom control with more natural reinforcers such as praise. The best way to accomplish this is to precede the delivery of tangible or activity reinforcers with praise or another social event. A teacher could compliment a student's behavior or pat him on the back before awarding him free time. If this is done consistently, the social events eventually become conditioned reinforcers and the use of tangible and activity reinforcers can be withdrawn, while the improvement is maintained.

We can go further with this. A visitor to your classroom should hear the air filled with compliments to individual children and the whole class. Too frequently, a teacher's main means of interacting with students is with reprimands and criticism. The students respond with nasty comments, and everyone loses. As mentioned before, praising students is a win–win situation. Students enjoy being in a classroom in which they are praised, and teachers enjoy teaching in this manner. The classroom atmosphere is happy and productive, and a close bond often forms between the students and the teacher. I have heard some teachers say to each other, "Don't smile until Christmas." The implication is that smiling and other kindnesses will be misinterpreted as teacher weakness. I could not disagree more. I say, "Start smiling after Labor Day and keep smiling until Flag Day." Try using praise at a high rate the next time you enter a classroom. When it starts working, it will become a wonderful addiction.

Question 21

How can you establish something as a conditioned reinforcer?

FINAL EXAMINATION

1. What are the characteristics of a well-defined behavior? Give a definition of out-of-seat behavior that meets these characteristics.

2. What is the purpose of a functional assessment? Name three possible functions of a behavior.

3. What is baseline? Indicate two measures a teacher can use to assess baseline.

    a. _____

35

b. _____

4. What are the characteristics of an appropriate intervention?

5. Why is it important to collect and graph data on out-of-seat behavior?

6. When is it necessary to revise an intervention?

7. On a separate sheet of paper, describe a flow chart depicting each of the steps in modifying behavior.

8. How can a teacher determine whether something is a positive reinforcer?

9. Describe three ways in which a teacher can identify a potential positive reinforcer.

   a.

   b.

   c.

10. What is wrong with claiming in advance that a particular event is a positive reinforcer for a student?

11. Identify five social, activity, and tangible events that can serve as potential reinforcers. Do not use any of the examples given in this book.

   Social   a. _____

             b. _____

             c. _____

             d. _____

             e. _____

   Activity a. _____

             b. _____

             c. _____

             d. _____

             e. _____

   Tangible a. _____

             b. _____

             c. _____

             d. _____

             e. _____

12. Distinguish between an individual contingency and a group contingency.

   _____

   _____

   _____

   _____

   _____

   _____

13. Distinguish between DRL and response cost.

14. Distinguish between DRO and unpredictable timings.

15. Discuss the advantages and disadvantages of the daily report-card procedure.

16. Name three adjustments not described in this book that a teacher can take to make a procedure more effective.

   a. _____

   _____

   b. _____

   _____

   c. _____

   _____

17. What are four behavior problems you have or are likely to encounter in the classroom? Prioritize them in the order of importance for behavior change.

   a. _____

   _____

   b. _____

   _____

   c. _____

   _____

   d. _____

   _____

18. Describe or hypothesize a situation in which out-of-seat behavior is a problem. Describe a procedure that might modify the behavior. Indicate how you would set the original criterion for reinforcement and how you might later change it.

   _____

   _____

   _____

   _____

   _____

19. Describe a program for decreasing out-of-seat behavior and the cues you would provide to increase the likelihood that students will perform the behavior successfully.

20. Describe a sequence of steps for teaching a student to imitate the behavior of asking for permission to leave his or her seat.

21. How can you establish something as a conditioned reinforcer?

ANSWER KEY

1. A well-defined behavior is observable, precise, and inclusive. Answers to the second part will vary.

2. The purpose of a functional assessment is to determine the reason a person performs a behavior. Three possible functions of a behavior are (a) to acquire attention, (b) to get out of doing an unpleasant assignment, or (c) to acquire a desired item.

3. Baseline is the measure of a behavior under normal conditions. A teacher can note (a) the number of times a behavior occurs or (b) the percentage of time it is occurring.

4. An appropriate intervention is one that is easy to apply, inexpensive, and has been effective with other students.

5. It is important to collect and graph data on out-of-seat behavior to let a teacher know whether a procedure is effective, to reinforce successful teacher efforts, and to communicate effectively with other educators and parents.

6. It is necessary to revise a procedure when it is ineffective, inconvenient, or expensive.

7. See Figure 3.

8. A teacher can claim something is a positive reinforcer if it increases the rate of a behavior that it follows.

9. Three ways to identify a potential reinforcer are to (a) present two or more reinforcers and have a student choose one, (b) ask the student to list and rank reinforcers, and (c) note what a student spends a lot of time doing.

10. A particular event cannot be classified as a reinforcer unless it increases the rate of a behavior that it follows.

11. Answers will vary.

12. In an individual contingency, a student's performance determines the individual reinforcer he or she will receive. In a group contingency, the behavior of all students determines the amount of reinforcement all students receive.

13. In DRL, students receive the entire reinforcer for keeping inappropriate behaviors below a certain criterion. They lose the entire reinforcer for exceeding the criterion. In response cost, students lose a portion of the reinforcer for each misbehavior.

14. In DRO, a behavior is reinforced only if it is appropriate for an entire interval. With unpredictable timings, behavior is reinforced, if it is appropriate, at the instance at which the timer goes off.

15. The advantages of daily report cards are that they cost the teacher nothing; they allow for awarding more powerful reinforcers than are available in school; they do not upset students who are not receiving extra reinforcers; and they improve communications between home and school. The disadvantages are that they can be used by parents as a reason to punish their children's behavior and that parents do not always carry out the procedures properly.

16. Answers will vary.

17. Answers will vary.

18. Answers will vary.

19. Answers will vary.

20. The teacher would model the correct behavior, prompt the student to imitate the behavior, and reinforce closer and closer approximations of the desired behavior.

21. Something can be established as a conditioned reinforcer by pairing it with another reinforcer.

FURTHER READINGS

Alberto, P. A., & Troutman, A. C. (2003). *Applied behavior analysis for teachers.* Upper Saddle River, NJ: Merrill.

Axelrod, S. (1987). Functional and structural analyses of behavior: Approaches leading to reduced use of punishment procedures? *Research in Developmental Disabilities, 8,* 165–178.

Axelrod, S. (1998). *How to use group contingencies.* Austin, TX: PRO-ED.

Axelrod, S., & Hall, R. V. (1999). *Behavior modification: Basic principles* (2nd ed.). Austin, TX: PRO-ED.

Barrish, H. H., Saunders, M., & Wolf, M. M. (1969). Good behavior game: Effects of individual contingencies for group consequences on disruptive behavior in a classroom. *Journal of Applied Behavior Analysis, 2,* 119–124.

Dietz, S. M., & Repp, A. C. (1973). Decreasing classroom misbehavior through the use of DRL schedules of reinforcement. *Journal of Applied Behavior Analysis, 6,* 457–463.

Dougherty, E. H., & Dougherty, A. (1977). The daily report card: A simplified and flexible package for classroom management. *Psychology in the Schools, 14,* 191–195.

Drew, B. M., Evans, J. H., Bostow, D. E., Geiger, G., & Drash, P. W. (1982). Increasing assignment completion and accuracy using a daily report card procedure. *Psychology in the Schools, 19,* 540–547.

Hall, R. V., & Hall, M. L. (1998a). *How to select reinforcers* (2nd ed.). Austin, TX: PRO-ED.

Hall, R. V., & Hall, M. L. (1998b). *How to use systematic attention and approval* (2nd ed.). Austin, TX: PRO-ED.

O'Neil, R. E., Horner, R. H., Albin, R. W., Sprague, J. R., Storey, K., & Newton, J. S. (1997). *Functional assessment and program development for problem behavior: A practical handbook.* Pacific Grove, CA: Brooks/Cole.

Proctor, M. A., & Morgan, D. (1991). Effectiveness of a response cost lottery raffle procedure on the disruptive classroom behavior of adolescents with behavior problems. *School Psychology Review, 20,* 97–109.

Sulzbacher, S. I., & Houser, J. E. (1968). A tactic to eliminate disruptive behaviors in the classroom: Group contingent consequences. *American Journal of Mental Deficiency, 73,* 88–90.

Van Houten, R., & Thompson, C. (1976). The effects of explicit timing on math performance. *Journal of Applied Behavior Analysis, 9,* 227–230.

Witt, J. C., & Elliot, S. N. (1982). The response-cost lottery: A time efficient and effective classroom intervention. *Journal of School Psychology, 20,* 155–161.

Wolf, M. M., Hanley, E. L., King, L. A., Lachowicz, J., & Giles, D. K. (1970). The timer-game: A variable interval contingency for the management of out of seat behavior. *Exceptional Children, 37*(2), 113–117.

ABOUT THE AUTHOR

Saul Axelrod is a professor of education in the Department of Curriculum, Instruction, and Technology in Education at Temple University. He received his doctorate from Florida State University and was a postdoctoral research fellow at the University of Kansas. His major interests include applying behavior analysis principles to the problems of managing classrooms and increasing the academic development of children from lower income families. Dr. Axelrod has served on the editorial boards of several journals, including the *Journal of Behavior Analysis, Journal of Behavioral Education, Child and Family Behavior Therapy,* and *Behavior Modification.* He is the author of numerous journal articles. He is the author or editor of *Behavior Modification for the Classroom Teacher, The Effects of Punishment on Human Behavior, Behavior Analysis and Treatment,* and *How To Use Group Contingencies.* He is also cofounder of the Delaware Valley Association for Behavior Analysis.

Use the new, fast-and-free, "orders only" fax number. 1-800-FXPROED
PRO-ED, 8700 Shoal Creek Boulevard, Austin, Texas 78757-6897   1-800/897-3202

Credit Card/PO Billing Address

Name _____

Address _____

_____

_____

Ship To: Telephone Number _____

Name _____

Address _____

_____

_____

GUARANTEE

All products are sold on 30-day approval. If you are not satisfied, you can return any product within 30 days. Please contact our office to receive authorization and necessary shipping instructions for returns. Prepaid orders will receive prompt refund, less handling charges. **Please use our fax number (1-800-FXPROED or 1-800/397-7633)!**

PAYMENT: All orders must be prepaid in full in U.S. funds by check or money order payable to PRO-ED, Inc., or by credit card. Open accounts are available to bookstores, public schools, libraries, institutions, and corporations. Please prepay first order and send full credit information to open an account.

Billing Authorization (must be completed or we cannot bill)

Purchase Order Number _____

❑ Payment Enclosed

Credit Card ❑ VISA ❑ MasterCard ❑ AMEX ❑ Discover

NOTE: Credit card billing address at top left must be completed if your order is charged to a credit card.

Authorized Signature _____

Card Number _____

Expiration Date _____

If prices on your order are incorrect, we reserve the right to exceed the amount up to 10% unless otherwise stated on your order. Terms are net, F.O.B. Austin, Texas; prices are subject to change without notice. ALL ORDERS MUST BE PAID IN U.S. FUNDS.

Quantity	Prod. No.	Book Title	Unit Price	Total
	10467	*How To Help Students Remain Seated*	$ 9.00	
	10468	*How To Deal Effectively with Lying, Stealing, and Cheating*	$ 9.00	
	10469	*How To Prevent and Safely Manage Physical Aggression and Property Destruction*	$ 9.00	
	10470	*How To Help Students Complete Classwork and Homework Assignments*	$ 9.00	
	10471	*How To Help Students Play and Work Together*	$ 9.00	
	10472	*How To Deal with Students Who Challenge and Defy Authority*	$ 9.00	
	10473	*How To Deal Effectively with Whining and Tantrum Behaviors*	$ 9.00	
	10474	*How To Help Students Follow Directions, Pay Attention, and Stay on Task*	$ 9.00	
	10465	All 8 *How To* titles	$56.00	

Product Total _____

Handling, Postage, and Carrying Charges
(U.S. add 10%; Canada add 15%; others add 20%. Minimum charge $1.00) _____

Subtotal _____

Texas residents ONLY add 8.25% sales tax or WRITE IN TAX-EXEMPT NUMBER _____

Grand Total (U.S. Funds Only) _____

PRO-ED, Inc.   8700 Shoal Creek Boulevard   Austin, Texas 78757-6897   Online store www.proedinc.com (secure server)

NOTES

NOTES

NOTES

NOTES

ADVANCE PRAISE FOR
Against Cheap Grace in a World Come of Age

"I enjoy using Ralph Garlin Clingan's work in teaching my courses and workshops."
— *Melva Wilson Costen, Professor of Liturgical Studies Emeritus,* The Interdenominational Theological Center *(Atlanta, Georgia), and Contributing Editor,* The Journal of the Interdenominational Theological Center

"Ralph Garlin Clingan's research deserves broader exposure."
— *Scott Holland, Assistant Professor of Peace Studies and Cross Cultural Studies, Bethany Theological Seminary (Richmond, Indiana), and Contributing Editor,* Cross Currents Magazine: The Journal of the Association of Religion and Intellectual Life

"Clayton Powell's career as activist pastor (1908–1937) of the nation's largest black church, Abyssinian Baptist in New York City, is well documented. *Against Cheap Grace in a World Come of Age,* however, focuses on Powell's theological formation and preaching. For the first time, Powell's formative influence on the young Dietrich Bonhoeffer is discussed in detail. Ralph Garlin Clingan is a passionate and evocative scholar."
— *Kenneth Rowe, Professor of Church History, Drew University School (Madison, New Jersey), and Archives Librarian, The United Methodist Church*

"I only wish I had possessed Dr. Clingan's work when I wrote my book about Dietrich Bonhoeffer."
— *Josiah Ulysses Young, III, Associate Professor of Theology, Wesley Theological Seminary, Washington, D.C.*